There'll be comparisons aplenty—Gary Snyder, Leonard Cohen, Nick Cave, Paul Durcan, John Cooper Clarke—but Koyczan is staking out his own literary acreage for himself. Koyczan employs a mysterious light touch to rip open your ribcage. Allow it.

—**Colum McCann**, IMPAC finalist, author of *Dancer*

I found *Visiting Hours...* in a lovely little bookstore in Toronto. I picked it up and straight away was hooked. He has an ability to take you straight into the heart of what on the surface may seem like mundane actions but which turn out to be much more complex. He makes you feel the depth of love, joy and pain in everyday life. Love, after all, is in everything.

—**Joel Pott,** *The Guardian*

It all sounds like... something's coming ... a sound everyone asks for.

—**Gordon Downie,** *The Tragically Hip*

Shane swallowed the stage with the power of his verse, stepping from subdued deep hot sad love poetry to hip-hop power chord meta-meter, throttling the crowd with the weight of his rhymes, and effectively wiping the stage with us.

While on tour we received copies of his first book, *Visiting Hours...* which is all that Shane is live, as fast and cool, and now as thrillingly rich and moving. And so, a whole new generation of rhyme readers will be born.

—**Dave Bidini,** *Rheostatics,* from *The Globe & Mail*

Shane Koyczan is electrifying. It's a rare poet who can make his audience laugh and cry; this is a writer who will break your heart then heal it.

—**Val McDermid**, author of *Wire in the Blood*, adapted for SHOWCASE television

Shane's performance was absolutely mind blowing, life changing, and inspiring.

—**Charlie Dark**, Blacktronica (UK)

"... it's time to hand out a few awards. Best chairman: Ian Rankin. Best poetry reading: Shane Koyczan. Best superstar: Salman Rushdie."

—**David Robinson**, Literary Editor, The Scotsman, reviewing the Edinburgh International Book Festival

"Shane Koyczan's performance at the Edinburgh International Book Festival was one of the outstanding successes of our programme. (The audience) laughed, they were moved, they were enthralled."

—**Catherine Lockerbie**, Artistic Director, Edinburgh International Book Festival

Visiting Hours

by

Shane .L. Koyczan

First published 2005
Second Edition 2006
This Edition 2007

ISBN-13: 978-0-9738131-0-4
ISBN-10: 0-9738131-0-5

Editing and layout by Chrystalene Buhler. Cover by Matthew Bowen. Printed and bound in Canada.

Download mp3s of some of these poems at:
http://www.houseofparlance.com/VisitingHours/

Find us by mail at:

House of Parlance Media Inc.
202 - 1636 West 2nd Avenue
Vancouver, British Columbia
V6J 1H4

Find us online at:

www.houseofparlance.com

"It doesn't happen all at once," said the Skin Horse. "You become. It takes a long time. That's why it doesn't happen often to people who break easily, or have sharp edges, or who have to be carefully kept. Generally, by the time you are Real, most of your hair has been loved off, and your eyes drop out and you get loose in your joints and very shabby. But these things don't matter at all, because once you are Real you can't be ugly, except to people who don't understand."

— The Velveteen Rabbit, Margery Williams

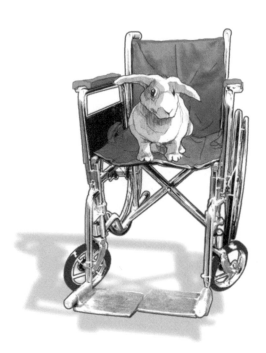

Contents

Foreword

I was excited when I heard that Shane Koyczan was releasing a book, for I always worried (a bit) that the muscle and sinew and (even) subtlety of his vision had been, so far, only experienced as sound. Shane Koyczan is a superb performance poet, but he is first and foremost a superb poet. Some of the depth and layering in Shane's crazy, looping narrative poems needed to be produced as text so readers could savour this thick, rich world he was making. It makes a whole lot of sense to me that a press would surface to give some of these new, exciting voices in contemporary poetry a body of text. From that point of view, *Visiting Hours* is a significant moment in Canadian poetry publishing.

Shane's long narrative poems have a trajectory that can be an amazing arc of vision. He begins, often, in the throw-away detritus of the textured, too-familiar surfaces of our lives. Airless small apartments or back alleys, booths in fast-food restaurants, the vague but powerful cages of suburban life with its thinly veiled hierarchies... all the huge, weary, jubilant imperfections of our wonderful lives and conversations. Then he takes us on a wild ride both into the heart of those things, that texture, and out of the heart of those things. At its edges, he forces us to peer back and realize that we do not have to accept their limits.

That's what I love about poems like "Visiting Hours," "Help Wanted," or the visceral, frank, obnoxious, crude and beautiful love poems... the way Shane tackles sexuality, the edginess and risks taken in that content. In this sense I see Koyczan's poems in a long line of voices including William Carlos

Williams, Henry Miller, Anaïs Nin, Jack Kerouac, William Burroughs, Thomas Pynchon, Louis Ferdinand Celine, Kurt Vonnegut, Joseph Heller, Tom Waits, Charles Bukowski, Tom Wayman, Dennis Lee, Evelyn Lau, Gordon Downie, Karen Solie and others surfacing around us.

As far as form is concerned, there have been instances when I have realized, while watching Shane, that he has pushed his own writing to a vehicle that carries his content perfectly. It sets up slowly, with a self-deprecating, smooth, deceptive simplicity of rhythm and narrative. Then, like the music of Sonny Rollins or Bill Evans, it improvises out of that narrative into an almost impossibly wide tableau of phrasing. It loses itself in wordplay, puns and visions, plays the complexity of our lives back at us like a beautiful wind, great gusts of riffs of our lives. That technical achievement reminds me of what Williams wanted to discover in modern poetics: a loose, but strongly cadenced, line that could speak in our real rhythms, could sing the complicated, often contradictory sounds of our lives, dancing in the dark and light of chaos as we manufacture our own love and dignity.

Gasp, chortle, wheeze, dribble, hack, whew! etc., etc. It isn't easy to simplify what Shane is achieving in the discipline of his craft. I want to thank Chrystalene Buhler for asking such a crusty old teacher and writer to try to say a few words about Shane Koyczan and his work, and I want to congratulate House of Parlance Media on this initiative. *Visiting Hours* is a stunning debut from an exciting new press in this country.

--John Lent, author of Monet's Garden and *So It Won't Go Away*

For the teachers
who have been my friends

For the friends
who have been my family

For the family
who I love

6:59 am

I've been told
that people in the army
do more by 7:00 am
than I do
in an entire day

but if I wake
at 6:59 am
and turn to you
to trace the outline of your lips
with mine
I will have done enough
and killed no one
in the process.

Skin 3

The night we met
was the first night I stopped making comparisons
left the ghost of an ex-lover
tap-tap-tapping on the window
as if a sheet of glass was enough to say
no
you can't come in tonight
we left the light on
because I had to see you for who you were
and who you were
was not her
which was a comfort
beyond all measure of comparison

skin tells you how to touch it
if you listen
and yours has been yelling
telling stories of yes and no
stop and go slow
like a snail that knows
the next rainfall
is at least
a week away

I listen to your skin say
right there
as if there was where
goosebumps become speed bumps
my fingers become tree trunks
slowly growing into forests

skin becomes kindling
as we begin smoke-signalling
lips to move in
your mouth was a bargain bin
and I was looking for a deal
it was practically boxing day
when I heard your skin say
your clothes
were one hundred percent
off
and your concerns
were out of stock

I could listen to your skin talk
for the better part of a week
so long as it would speak to me of you
turning knowledge into a residue
whose value
is determined by how much pressure I apply
when I place my hands
where you want me to

few are the smiles
that I have sought
with such relentlessness
as if to dismiss
all other aspects of my life
focus on now
and how it is you came to be
an answer to the question
I asked myself
the last time I was alone

I've grown from the head down
refusing to plant my feet on the ground
because only statues were made
to stand still

I will walk to you
so long as I can hear your skin say
you've got my back like vertebrae.

Jason Bionic

He looks at himself
in the mirror
every morning

he ponders duplexes
imagines that they must be ashamed
of how they look
then kisses his metal biceps

he glances at two pieces of bread
and suddenly
they are toast

he returns to his bedroom
wakes up his girlfriend
by vibrating his tongue
2 million times a second

on mornings like these
when his girlfriend's legs
are wrapped around his head
tighter than the pucker
of a baby tasting its first lemon
he becomes thankful
his skull is reinforced with titanium

on mornings like these
he runs laps
around the cherry trees
until the blossoms fall loose

and all that can be seen
is a whirlwind of pink petals
taking the shape of a giant heart
outside his girlfriend's bedroom window

on mornings like these
he is happy

but on mornings
when his legs
are not fast enough
to save a puppy
from being hit by a buick
   on mornings
when his arms
are not strong enough
to push a beached whale
back into the ocean
   on mornings
when the lasers in his eyes
are not hot enough
to melt a frozen lake
and save a young girl
trapped under the ice

on mornings like these
he cries

because he is bionic

and it is the very least
he can do.

Pulse

What I said was
I'll miss you
what I meant to say was
I love you
what I wanted to say was
that I meant what I said
and it's funny
how all those things I
could have said
flooded my head after we said goodbye
and I should have told you
I'd be willing to hold you
until my flesh crumbles into bone
because I'm willing to die alone
but god knows I don't want to live that way
because some say that the highway
becomes a flat line
if you travel it for too long
and I can't tell if they're wrong
I've seen the strong
fall to their knees and beg please
for some strength because the length of one bad day
had them ready to throw their arms up at life and say
I quit
I mean I have seen some shit

seen the sun bake the gravel used
on interstates and intersections
into fun house mirrors

that cast reflections
of my three years on the road
when I slowed to get directions
just looking for someone to hold
they were all happy
to point away from themselves
and say "maybe down the road somewhere"
who knew that you'd be there
who knew that they were right
that my flag is a traffic light
at night it glows
red amber and green
and I've seen them everywhere
so I guess in that sense
the road really is my home
but I've got poem after poem
of what it's like to miss
a home cooked meal
of what it's like to wake up and feel
my arm draped over your absence
how I miss breathing in your skin
like incense
I bet you never knew
that when I'm sleeping beside you
I wake up just to make sure I'm holding
you
feel like a mountain
that doesn't know it's being climbed
as your breath is timed with the in and out of mine
I run my hand up your spine
like it was the centreline of a highway
with no stop sign

I hit the intersection
where your shoulders meet your neck
passing the car wrecks of ex-boyfriends
who parallel parked on the dead ends
and I just hope your skin
lends me an extra mile
so I can slow down
take a while to admire the landscape
drape my arm over your being there this time
when it comes to your skin
I'm a drunk driver trying to walk a straight line

I've been pulled over so much
that your simple touch is enough to make me
assume the position
wishing I could stay there
where your hand searches my body for the contraband
that could land me in the jail of your ribcage
because road rage is a sickness
and my medicine is your skin
so I'm constantly getting myself in trouble
double parking beside you
merging with the changing lanes
of each other's veins
all highways leading back to one heart
because I end where you start
I could spend the rest of my life
circling the same block
wondering
where does the world hide its private stock of people like you
and why do I get to be the lucky one
who learns how to do back to u-turns

and some days collapse on me
like the night
I can tell I haven't slept
when the light peeks through the blinds
and finds me
with my eyes wide open
hoping I can take all these poems
I printed on post-it notes
fold them into tiny boats and launch them
towards the shores of your skin
where they begin to colonize
take root in your eyes
weigh anchor in the harbour of your thighs
until all the tiny hairs on your body
begin to rise
like a million flags brought to mast
at long last
I know I no
longer have to roam
and I finally understand those sailors
who plant their lips to the ground
I do the same to your body
it's because you taste like home

and
what I said was
I'll miss you
what I meant to say was
I love you
what I wanted to say was
that I meant what I said

I miss you like I miss my own bed
after too many nights of sleeping on couches
and hardwood floors
or sitting silently behind the doors of hotel rooms
that become wombs
breathing a life into this loneliness
I miss you like a burn victim
must miss their own skin
I miss you like a sad ending
must miss some place new to begin
because some say that the highway
becomes a flat line
if you travel it for too long
I can't tell if that's true or false
but I'm racing down it towards you
trying to find my pulse.

Quiet Man

Quiet man's power
is a bit complicated

he eats his burrito
quietly
and thinks about the hands
that made it for him

he has faith that they were washed
that the little sign in the bathroom
posted by the management
and the bottle of discount liquid soap
have both been noted and put to use

he peels away more of the tin foil
taking another bite
and he remembers his friend
telling him "pollo"...means chicken
and he feels cultured
in a very small
and matter of fact way

he takes another large bite and his server
blonde hair blue eyes large breasts and shapely legs
asks him "is everything alright?"

he keeps his mouth shut
wipes hot sauce from his lips
then gives her the somewhat awkward thumbs up
that is reserved for every server

with the unearthly sense of timing to ask you a question
when your mouth is full

he could say
the crickets have arthritis
he could say
I love you
to break the silence
could tell her that
there are jellyfish
that would grow spines
just for an opportunity
to walk on land
stop at her feet
and kiss her toes

but
he just nods his head
and lets the interruption pass
quietly
like the stork that broke its neck
delivering a one-ton baby
to a one-pound single father
who knew enough of faith and fortune
to keep his mouth shut.

On My Back

We don't know if chicken little
was right

the sky really is falling
and us right along with it
                falling at the same
speed and time
to give the illusion
        of never falling at all
    don't know if some true ground
is rushing up to meet us

so I leave you to get on top
as I lie on my back for you
because reality comes hard
and perhaps I can cushion the blow
for one of us

we are dealing from a deck of cards
where the diamonds hearts clubs and spades
are now
most likelys probablys maybes
and maybe knots
that have left us in the hopeless tangle
of each other
like the tendrils of jellyfish
tied together at the ends
while we pull in opposite directions
creating a net that has caught silence
and kept it tightly between us

we don't know if we are two separate dreams
growing into one another
in the long sleep
of some lonely god
who loves the quiet eyes of misery
because it's all he knows

but there is something
                something about the way
the clouds are moving
that tells me
we are falling

so I lie on my back for you.

My Darling Sara

The failing use of my right hand
isn't actually the failing use of my right hand
it's just another way to tell the time
and I'm ticking
so I've been picking myself up at bars
with a bottle in each hand
but I never give myself any play
I only make plans with myself for the day after next
but by the time the sun swings back around into position
I forget the context of why I asked myself out
in the first place

did I think I was going to score?

I let a stranger pour me one more
she says
my name is Sara

doesn't take much more than that
to start a relationship

my darling Sara
cleans rooms for a living
giving her youth and beauty
to dirt and dust
understands more than most
that family must be a foot you put forward first
you must weather the worst together
but having never met her family
she places love above all else

then protests that I use the word love
too freely in poems
and I should really just say what I mean

and I suppose what I mean most is that
I'm trying

she's been buying me time
on a maxed-out credit card
arms scarred from selling her own blood
to pay down the debt
tells me she doesn't mind going broke
just so long as I can give her a little sweat
she says
try

so I do my best impression
of a pen
and when every problem looks like a page
I commit ink to paper
the worth of the words that come out
determines my wage
I've been making enough
to pay her the compliment
of not quitting
of not sitting
when standing is required
she only asks that I put the effort in
and in return she's willing
to pin a paper heart to her chest
then do her best impression
of a target

Sara tells me that effort
is the Siamese twin of success
so when everyone else looks like a wrong answer
she says she'll settle for being my best guess

so we lie in bed like a mess
that someone's been meaning to clean
for the large part
of a long while
we lie there like a pile of dirty laundry
and how we'll ever come clean
is beyond me
so we don't

she says
it's supposed to be dirty
if by the end you haven't hurt me
then you didn't try

so I do my best impression
of a surgeon
cutting purple hearts out of my own
use my veins like thread
then have hurt sewn to our skin like medals
because when the bleeding stops
and that dust settles
all we have are our wounds
to wear like decorations
upon our chests

Sara does her best impression of a war
tells me not to count my pride among the casualties

because maybe faith means never keeping score
she says there's more to effort than just switching gears
and in terms of what one should give in this life
sweat holds more value than tears

you have to try
and even though
the failing use of my right hand
means I'll never land a knockout punch
in the first round
life is composed of sound and fury
whatever noise is left in me
will be twice as loud when I try
so I plug myself into the idea of going the distance
and I amplify

Sara has a throat like a vase
she sings her words into bloom
has a voice like perfume
it's been sticking to my clothes
so everyone knows where I've been sleeping

she's been keeping me so close
you could use my body for evidence
pull her fingerprints as proof
that she's been on top so often
she's starting to look like my roof

but a real sexy roof
and she doesn't leak

unless you count the crying

she does that sometimes
worries that she's just a back-up plan
but I've lived long enough to learn
too many options can kill a man
I will make no exodus
I'll be around long enough
to watch uncertainty bid us farewell
then echo our names into the crater
caused by the impact
of when our lack of conviction fell

Sara
you've never had to sell me on the idea
of absolute certainty in the trustworthiness of another
the first and only time you met my mother
mom said
"I like the way she looks at you"
and I echoed back to her
that I liked it too

eyes like recycle-bin blue
Sara looks at broken things
as if she can make them new
more than a few times I've caught her staring
                              caught her wearing
a smile reserved for those busy making plans

Sara believes that distance is a fundamental
that can be side-stepped by a piece of string
and two tin cans

and I remember when my tin can rang

they said
there's no family to speak of
so love is next in line
and there's not a lot of time but
she's asking for her boyfriend

in the cab to the hospital I feel my heart bend
as if bracing for impact
so I do my best impression of a man
and face fact

it's supposed to hurt

a doctor does his best impression of the truth
and spares me his attempts to skirt around the issue

they can't stop the bleeding

and the failing use of Sara's heart
isn't actually
        the failing use of Sara's heart
it's just another way to tell the time
and she's ticking

my darling Sara
I was holding your hand when you died
and even though the failing use of my right hand
prevented me from feeling you leave

I tried.

2 Seconds

I remember
the second
I started loving you

it was the second
before I wrote you this poem.

Visiting Hours

During visiting hours
I had to read to sick people

people who had no one

it was my punishment
catholic school community service
for farting on a nun's muffin

it was an accident I swear to god

and every day would start the same way
she'd say
"how are you doing?"
and I'd say "I'm doing alright"
she'd say "I'm doing just fine"

point in fact
the cancer had taken both of her breasts
but she could laugh
      she had a laugh like a welcome mat
she wore the same kind of smile
curious george would wear
if he finally came out of the closet
to be with the man in the big yellow hat

she'd touch where they used to be
and say "it's probably good that they're gone
my ex used to go about them all wrong
half the time the only reason my nipples were erect

was because they were trying to jump off of my body
to run away from his tongue"

I was thirteen years young
thinking to myself
"oh my god you're awesome"

for me it was all about visiting hours
I hadn't read to her in days
she was too busy teaching me
how to watch horror movies and laugh
because all of the monsters Hollywood can think up
just aren't as scary
as letting yourself be talked into
believing you can be only half of what you are
she'd put a hand on each scar
and say "if you really want to get scared
watch the news"

it's a steeplechase
every day thousands of people face
going under thousands of knives
but it's still more cost-effective
for doctors to pay off lawsuits
than it is to save lives

"so don't try walking a mile in my shoes
just wear my pyjamas
and walk in my dreams instead
because this isn't a deathbed
I'm not gonna give up today
I'm not just gonna lay here and take it

because sometimes life is as elusive
as getting an orgasm from my ex
sometimes I just got to fake it
so if anyone ever tells you
you're not good enough
you're not smart enough
give up your foolish dream
if anyone ever tells you to quit
you got to make them wear a diaper on their mouth
because man they're just talking shit"

I was thirteen years young
two thoughts
one... marry me
two... she talks a lot about how bad sex with her ex was
she says it's because it's true
"he was like a rubik's cube
too hard to figure out
and twenty years out of style"
then she'd smile and say
"you gotta let your body be the rocking chair
that soothes the tired body of hope
    let your arms be the rope
around the neck of self-loathing
    let your skin be the clothing
that keeps compassion warm
on the cold streets of regret"
she says "don't pray for me yet"

and I said "no problem
religion is something I gave up on
along with dieting

but love
	love is a feeling that in me and through me
I've often called god
so I will love you "

she looked me straight in the heart and said
"that's why I'm glad
they don't make hospital beds for two
because kid you
got your own shit to do
and I can't continue
to let you be doing alright
or be doing just fine
not when there's a world full of people
who are tired of dressing in shadows
just waiting for you to shine

"now bring me my goddamn jello"

she liked jello
she liked me too

during visiting hours
I had to read to the people
who had no one
but this is about a woman named everyone
this isn't about death
it's about the fact
that I can still feel her breath in my ear
sometimes I can even hear her say
"you're not giving up today"

because I live in a world
full of seeing-eye underdogs
and I'm pretty sure
we're all tired of wearing our choke chains
we're tired of being treated like walking canes
in a world so blind
no one can find the other
so we just keep bumping into one another
as if people are just buildings made of bone
who collapse every time they're made to believe
they were meant to stand alone
but you're not

some of us can love

and yeah
some of us are going to get cancer
and some of us are going to fall in our showers
but until then you've got to shine
because all the time you get
it's just visiting hours.

Thought Lines

You called them your thought lines
those little wrinkles that ran across your forehead
when you were deep in thought

and I thought you should know

when you're sleeping
there are no trenches
running across your forehead
where your thoughts
gather to take on the world

and later
when you wake you will speak to me
of the men using baby seals for batting practice
in the arctic circle
of the politicians who carry smashed atoms
inside of their briefcases

and later
I will point to the evening clouds
and tell you that they are
pastel pink and orange dragons
perched on the horizon
reading bedtime stories to the sun

and later
when you close your eyes

you will dream of children
planting bullets in the ground
hoping to grow trees
that can defend themselves against lumberjacks

and you will smile
having for a moment
forgotten about the world's daily business

and later
when you wake
you will ask me why I'm smiling
and I will tell you
because it's okay to be happy

and I thought you should know.

Finally

Boyfriend man is so glad
your dad hates him

he's finally the dangerous man
he always wanted to be.

The Ultimate Love Poem

If I were a cow
en route to the slaughterhouse
I would try to kiss you
one last time
before my lips were mulched for wieners.

Skin 1

Skin
continuously rolls away from us
like burnt-out tractor tires
that wobble to a
standstill
that will build the foundation for empires
and dynasties
whose histories are written in books
bound by our spines
where there will be no lines to read between
because we've been
filling in the spaces
with the hope
that truth retraces its steps
to find that it was always standing still
and will remain statuesque
until we are brave enough to make promises
so this is mine

I will pride myself on the title
best friend
slit my wrists
on your shoulder blades
allowing my pulse to lend life
to every dead end
then bend my breath
to the shape of your heartbeat
and meet you to make noise
at the silences in between

where honesty is the foreplay
that prompts us to finally come clean

because honestly
I've been thinking of holding your hand

as I am tired of holding my breath
or tongue
I will task each rib into a rung
leaving ladders
that lead to the top of each lung
so you can witness
where all of my words for you hung
at the gallows of my own cowardice.

Afraid

In the director's cut
of the movie of my life
you're the eternity
of never-before-seen footage
and I just want my eyesight to get worse
I want to cancel my prescriptions
so I can go blind
and learn to see the world through your descriptions
I could spend all night renewing my subscriptions
to your skin
because your articles are better written in braille
who needs the latest issue of time
when I could find forever
in the hourglass of your body

I could build a future between your thighs
then look into your eyes trying to find
my own private history channel
with a lifelong documentary
on whether or not this was meant to be
and I don't want to turn any of this into poetry
but
you're so beautiful
flowers turn their heads to smell you

and when I'm all alone
I'm rifling through the pockets
in the back of my mind
trying to find spare excuses
so I can call you on the phone

and it's strange
the way I need a reason
just to call you up and say
that I thought about you today
the way your hair spirals down
like corkscrews made of solid silk
yesterday I saw a picture of truth
on the back of a carton of milk
it was missing
and I'd like to look for it
in the lost-and-found of your lips
because truth be told
I'd rather be kissing

but I am afraid
of what you'd say
if I told you
that I like you
and not in a friendly way
I know it sounds cliché
but if life is a highway
and we're just barreling down it
in an out-of-control car
then I want to hold onto you
like you were the "oh shit" bar
because I am afraid

see
my life was so much simpler
way back when I could just disappear
but now it's like
I want to press my ear to your ear

like two seashells trying to hear
the sounds of the ocean
this emotion rolling in and out like
breathi
                    in and out like
breathi
                    in and out like
breathing

I've loved women
like I was only a breath of air
necessary but so unnoticed
it was like I was never there
but with you

goddamn

I am a serial lover
leaving behind fingerprints
like they were evidence
that I was there
leaving behind strands of my hair
on your sweater
when I hug you goodbye
I am slowly becoming a fact

and I'm afraid
that I'll be tracked back
to the days when I was like popeye
without the spinach
because even now sometimes I feel
like I'm just one enormous achilles heel

I keep having nightmares
that someone is trying to steal
my life right out from under me
it's got me curling up into foetal position
wishing I could dream some way into your arms
but the problem with dreams
is that all the alarms start ringing
like they were singing
  the sound of the music I have to face
like the sound of the music I have to face
is the morning
adorning me with the reality
that maybe

you're not looking for anyone right now

but how many more uses
can we invent out of the excuses
that "I'm sorry… we should just be friends"
because
times are tough
things are rough
all of those apologies that made us feel
like we were never beautiful enough
when beautiful is all we ever wanted to be

I would chop down my own family tree
to make paper and write out
a hundred different poems
explaining how beautiful you are to me
like your skin is where silkworms gather
to understand things like softness

you know I could go on
but I've been aboard that friend ship
for so long that I'm seasick and vomiting
over the edge while dreaming of mutiny
we live our lives under the scrutiny of a world
that rewards confidence over eloquence
but if uncertainty is the only thing that's keeping us apart
I want to hop that fence
strip you down to your confusions
and spend all night making...
sense to you

because if we're not waiting

we're

hesitating

and I've lived my life
watching love slip through my hands like time
like the tick-tock of a
melting salvador dali clock
when I'm with you I stock every minute
as if by looking at it long enough
I could find eternity in it
and holding you
I would slit the wrists
on the hands of a clock
if I thought it could make that moment
last forever
my life became a bumper sticker
the moment I met you

it's true

shit actually happens

and I am afraid
that I've strayed
so far down the shopping aisle
I've watched stock boys file true love
under relationships in a can
I'm not sure there is a grand plan

I've seen a praying mantis lose faith

but I want to believe that you think about me
when I'm not around
and that the sound of my voice on the phone
is enough to reassure you
that if you're feeling afraid
it's okay

you're not so completely alone.

Elephant Man

The beautiful woman held his hand
the same way a child holds the string
that holds the helium balloon
that holds the child's sense
of wonder
and holding her hand

he felt like the star
some lover in a distant land
must be wishing on tonight

but the boy
    the boy with the perfect sideburns
and hair like the shavings left
on god's workshop floor
after carving the sun
laughed at her
said he was ugly
and walked on smiling

suddenly the star he was went supernova
and the wish made by some lover in a distant land
came true

and he remembers
    remembers the elephant
who hoped for a peanut but instead
had a cigarette extinguished on its trunk

12 years later a man who 12 years prior
had extinguished a cigarette on an elephant's trunk
was trampled to death by an elephant who remembered

and though he is not a violent man
for the boy with the perfect sideburns
he will be an elephant

placing his words on the boy's chest gently
like a grey one-ton leg
and letting the weight of them sink in
until the boy remembers
until lack of breath
forces the boy to apologize with his eyes

until the heart
stops.

Inside the Lines

She had
bad hair

the worst I've ever seen

and bad hair
was a disease
that affected mainly
grade-eight girls
with a need to be accepted

I went to junior high
in the age of hot-pink pants
and hip neon-green suspenders

the music of new kids on the block
taught us to take our relationships
"step by step"
and hairspray became the halo
for every girl
who wanted to be an angel
in the eyes
of a thirteen-year-old boy

we were staying inside the lines

in an attempt to fit in
she spent one morning
in front of a mirror
with every little girl's best friends

a blow-dryer
and a can of maximum hold

in grade eight
we studied mythology
the boys drew icarus
the girls drew pegasus
as hercules and I
found equality
in our inability to save the world
or even our fathers

and I'm not saying it happened
but like a child in a courtroom
who points out
the man who molested her
in a room
where the teddy bears watched
and the glowworms
faded into the darkness

she found the courage
to walk into class
hair vast enough
to rival the highest peak on mount olympus
ominous enough
to kill the kraken

fingers pointed at her
like sharpened pencils
promising to draw the points
and connect the dots

because opinions were the new toy
if our parents had them
we wanted them too
and we would lock her away within them

keep her inside the lines

sitting at her desk
with the eyes of every student
studying her
like an obscure literary reference
that everyone pretends to get
like a complicated mathematical equation
that no one really understands

example:

she applies half a can of hairspray
leaves her house at 9:37
walks the full four kilometres to school
because her single-parent father
can't afford to drive her
she eats one apple on the way to school
saves one for lunch
arrives in the middle of English class

and I'm not saying it happened
but how long was it before
every whisper behind her back
multiplied itself into another morning
in front of a mirror
with every pariah's best friends

intention
and a bottle of daddy's painkillers

the popular girls swung their heads
like pendulums
threatening to cut away
any hope of solving this problem

in grade eight we studied mythology
the kids called her medusa
and she must have wished it were true
everyone might have been
a little more careful
not to look her in the eyes
when insulting her

but no
they said she was out of place
like the dandelion that grows up
through the cracks in the cement

and she was
like that dandelion
beautiful

because it doesn't know
it's not supposed to grow there

by grade eight
we had unlearned our grace
the ability to use our arms
to draw new lines

around the shoulders of someone
whose skin colour was like a gift
brought to us by crayola
or
whose hair took the shape of the wind
if you could catch it
and place it on someone's head
like a crown

in grade eight
atlas and I found equality
in our inability to save the world
or even ourselves
I sat next to medusa

we drew lines out of there.

What They Never Told Me

The beautiful man
can tattoo a permanent twinkle
in the eye
of a young girl

the beautiful woman
can cause a young boy's tongue
to tidal-wave
inside his mouth
and flood his head
with daydreams

but when they believe
you are not beautiful
they will call you friend

they will grip tightly
the reins of your unattractiveness
using the morals
you have earned
by living a life of humility
to pull themselves through this world

they will call it loyalty

but the shoulder
you've put in
to carry their beauty
will shape you

strong enough
to snap the reins
strong enough
to walk away

when you do decide to leave
do not look back

they have snakes for hair

and will
turn you to stone.

For the Woman

... who told me to fuck off
after I told her she was beautiful

It doesn't matter
that you are a horrible person

you are the reason
that boys
dream of becoming astronauts
so they can
man the first mission to pluto
and carve an ice sculpture
that resembles you
then alien passers-by will know
that our planet
has its moments

p.s.

the aliens will probably masturbate
while thinking of you
then launch an invasion
to capture you for their king
when you tell him
to fuck off
the earth will be destroyed

I... only want to write poems.

Is It Me?

As per usual
the only seat
left on the bus
was the one
right beside koyczan

and what with koyczan being
the living embodiment
of every stereotype
that has ever been branded
into the fleshy love handles
of an obese person

she decided to stand
instead.

Etiquette

She looked like a joke

not funny

it was just that men kept falling for her
the same way children fall from trees
the same way trees fall in a forest
the same way forests fall
because chainsaws have politician tongues
that try to sound out words like
progress

maybe not the same way
but there was something very hollywood about her

walked in slow motion
talked like cigar smoke
dripping lazily
from the lips of someone important

she was terribly cliché
which I guess is what made me want to fuck her
in the first place

and yes
there is something horribly honest
about saying you want to fuck someone
the same way
there is something honest about
unflushed urinals

maybe not the same way
but there were no children dipped in my dna
looking at me from behind her eyes
and she in no way
reminded me of a sunset

because a sunset would never ask me
to meet in the bathroom
and I would never ask a sunset to go down

it does that on its own

and of course there is etiquette

for fucking
                    there is etiquette
for every situation
for example
if a woman presents herself to you as a joke
do not fall for her

laugh with her

then wait

and tell her to others.

Ego

I
find it almost impossible
to start a poem
without using the word
I
whenever
you
are involved

the word
me
seems to come up
more often than
I
would like but
I
can't talk about
you
without bringing
me
into it

this should be much simpler
like grade-one
problem-solving
but the problem is
you
are happiest when
I
fail and

I
know that
you
think that this is all about ego
        this is all about
me

so
I
find it impossible
to start a poem
using the word

we.

Diligence Man

Diligence man knows
exactly what she means
when she says
"I have rules"

it means his tongue
has no passport
his hand on her back
moving in a circular
counter-clockwise motion
in an attempt to rewind time
to a moment
before she made rules
is about
as welcome as
a high-school bully
at a dungeons & dragons convention

but he persists
as he is not one to
fight his own nature

she
knows exactly who he is
so when the word "respect"
falls out of his mouth
like half-chewed veal
and lands at her feet
like a dead mouse
from the mouth of a cat

she will let the scream
that has been bouncing around
in her lungs
hit the wall of her teeth
and do her best
to smile politely

but a polite smile
is all the invitation he needs
a few more drinks
and diligence man
becomes compliment slut
he will liken her eyes to something beautiful
but soon correct himself
when he realizes
that beautiful people
know they are beautiful
and would prefer to hear
how intelligent they are

they believe that wit
is the siamese twin of magnificence

so he will mention politics
    he will nod his head
to her observations about the world's
current political climate
and let his eyes say
"wow... I never really looked at it like that"
which is technically true
seeing as he has never really looked at it
ever

the amazing thing about compliment slut
is that he remains diligent
        he can force himself
to believe things
like the look on her face is merely indigestion
like her moving away isn't actually her moving away
it's just being shy
like her hand on her boyfriend's inner thigh
slowly moving back and forth
letting the friction
build heat
is really just her hand on her brother's inner thigh
slowly moving back and forth
as a show of affection
between family

but in the end
diligence man
will
move on

to someone else

as he is not one
to fight his own nature.

Hatchets

I've buried hatchets
in so many small american towns
that when I finally go to heaven or hell
I will be able to open a hardware store
specializing in hatchets
and I'll spend eternity
sharpening all of those axes
that I forgot to grind
along the way.

Restaurant

I met a man who makes meals at a restaurant
where there's no menu
but everything's on it
impossible
I know
but I met a man who makes meals at a restaurant
called death row
I met a man who makes the last meals
and I know way too many people
who would attack him asking him how it feels
to be part of something like that
so instead we just chew the fat
and I listen

he tells me about a 31-year-old boy
                    a 31-year-old boy
who was sentenced at the age of 22
waited nine years on death row
and last week was his turn
so he asked for sourdough french toast
and a side of magic beans
because a boy would rather face down a giant
take his chances with a beanstalk
than walk down that hall
where every footfall echoes into that same oblivion
where every experience never had congregates
to create a world never lived in
a boy could find himself asking for things like magic beans
and a cook find himself understanding what it means
to be desperate

and he says
most of this food never gets touched
but that doesn't stop him from being exact
even though
he'll never make a meal like mom could
it'll never taste as good as it would
coming from the one who raised you
and he knows this
but he's meticulous
even though he knows that this 31-year-old boy
grabbed his arresting officer's service revolver
and tried to use it as a problem solver
he makes french toast with sourdough
as though he were cooking for a king
because the last thing you should do is eat well
especially if there's a family praying that you go slow
when you take that walk through hell
so everything's fresh
the eggs are free range
and there's a last-minute change of pans
because the last hands to wash that pan
missed a spot
this cook's got a vision of french toast
that falls apart so softly
it feels like lovers lying in bed breaking apart
to sleep
so deeply that the shallow of their dreams
is enough for hate to drown in
because if you're going to come up short
on a request like magic beans
you better be sure that the first part of that meal
means something

he says it's a job
and as cliché as it sounds
someone's got to do it
tells me that back in the day
they used to let mothers try
but most of them couldn't get through it
a job was born out of necessity
and those struck by poverty
didn't have false visions
of turning this work into their legacy
they didn't dream of a dynasty
where the mountains were made of chocolate
and sugar stood in for sand
but they knew america would put a cheque in their hand
so men and women were born into workers
because ideas like right and wrong get outweighed by need
any time you've got mouths to feed

he tells me that america failed
it nailed freedom to a cross
because every boss in every office
is their own separate world
held up on the backs of employees
who are expected to say please
every time they have to take a piss
and I know way too many people
who tell me it can't go on like this
and we say this
but we still set our alarms to be up in time
for our nine to five
we're just reporters coming to you live
from bus stops and coffee shops

we wear our lives like costumes
and use bills and coins like props
in an over-budget production
that we cannot seem to stop
so it just goes on like this
as if we accept this
as if we've all become buddhas of mass production
our brains rotting like teeth
under the sweet unending bliss
of false enlightenment
and he tells me that maybe we
used to be flint
and we'd spark when struck by new ideas
but now all there is
is jobs
and someone's got to do them
and isn't he lucky
that he lives in a country
where everyone wants to be someone

and isn't he lucky
that when the day's done
he can go home and forget
like he played his hand
knowing it was a bad bet
because "what you risk
reveals what you value"
and this man ventured everything he knew
to the point where his wife cannot convince him
that her eyes are the colour blue
because what life have you got left
if you want no one to know what you do

see
he lets everyone think
that he's just a cook because
he doesn't want his kids to know what daddy does
and is unable to tell his mother where he was
when they executed a 31-year-old boy
for killing the first son to the same mother

he made the meal for the man who took his brother
because he would not trust it
to anyone who was willing to fill in for him that day
because they'd say things like "don't worry"
with just enough of a smile
that if he ever stood trial
trying to defend that meal
all he'd ever feel was
guilty

so he made french toast with sourdough
as though he were making a monument to his virtues
that would never be brought down
by the half-truths of america

in truth it never got touched

he tells me when the skeletons in his closet
finally bust down the door
all he'll need is his fist and someone's jaw

regret is like living your life as a blind man
having to imagine
everything you lived but never saw

he can't picture it any different
than his mother at an execution
sitting in the front row
clear tears mixing with blush and eye shadow
looking as though
she'd been punched by a rainbow
but he says "I know I did the right thing"
no one will ever sing his praise
raise a big deal made of marble
or concrete
america will never fall to his feet
and say "I'm sorry"
all this is
is the story of a man who makes meals
one day
he made a testament to his ethics
golden brown and stacked a perfect five inches high
he tells me he feels bad for the boys on death row
who know america failed them

he says most of them still ask for apple pie.

Surprise

I found god
inside a cracker jack box

smaller than I expected.

Hardship Man

Hardship man has no heart
so he keeps love in his left kidney
somewhere deep inside of it
he knows
that every relationship will end badly

and in the divorce settlements that are sure to follow
he will get the photo albums
but a long line of exes will be awarded the memories
he will have to live his life
marvelling at how often he ate cake with strangers
and never knowing why it hurts so much to pee

and I don't want to jump to conclusions
I've never been athletic
but something tells me that hardship man's house
is overflowing with toasters
all of them the exact same model
received as gifts
and although hardship man loves toast
when the toasters are lined up in a row
he feels they are meant only to tease him
                    to hint at a series of failures

so
he keeps one by the bathtub
for that eventual night
when he finally realizes
he can't remember
why he even tried.

We Are More

When defining canada
you might list some statistics
you might mention our tallest building
or biggest lake
you might shake a tree in the fall
and call a red leaf canada
you might rattle off some celebrities
    might mention buffy sainte-marie
    might even mention the fact that we've got a few
barenaked ladies
or that we made these crazy things
like zippers
electric cars
and washing machines
when defining canada
it seems the world's anthem has been
"been there done that"
and maybe that's where we used to be at
it's true
we've done and we've been
           we've seen
all the great themes get swallowed up by the machine
and turned into theme parks
but when defining canada
don't forget to mention that we have set sparks

we are not just fishing stories
about the one that got away
we do more than sit around and say "eh?"
and yes

we are the home of the rocket and the great one
who inspired little number nines
and little number ninety-nines
but we're more than just hockey and fishing lines
off of the rocky coast of the maritimes
and some say what defines us
is something as simple as please and thank you
and as for you're welcome
well we say that too
but we are more
than genteel or civilized
we are an idea in the process
of being realized
we are young
we are cultures strung together
then woven into a tapestry
and the design
is what makes us more
than the sum total of our history
we are an experiment going right for a change
with influences that range from a to zed
and yes we say zed instead of zee
we are the colours of chinatown and the coffee of little italy
we dream so big that there are those
who would call our ambition an industry
because we are more than sticky maple syrup and clean snow
we do more than grow wheat and brew beer
we are vineyards of good year after good year
we reforest what we clear
because we believe in generations beyond our own
knowing now that so many of us
have grown past what used to be
we can stand here today

filled with all the hope people have
when they say things like "someday"

someday we'll be great
someday we'll be this
or that
someday we'll be at a point
when someday was yesterday
and all of our aspirations will pay the way
for those who on that day
look towards tomorrow
and still they say someday

we will reach the goals we set
and we will get interest on our inspiration
because we are more than a nation of whale watchers and lumberjacks
           more than backpacks and hiking trails
we are hammers and nails building bridges
towards those who are willing to walk across
we are the lost-and-found for all those who might find themselves at a
loss
we are not the see-through gloss or glamour
of those who clamour for the failings of others
we are fathers brothers sisters and mothers
uncles and nephews aunts and nieces
we are cousins
we are found missing puzzle pieces
we are families with room at the table for newcomers
we are more than summers and winters
           more than on and off seasons
we are the reasons people have for wanting to stay
because we are more than what we say or do
we live to get past what we go through

and learn who we are
        we are students
              students who study the studiousness of studying
so we know what as well as why
  we don't have all the answers
but we try
and the effort is what makes us more
we don't all know what it is in life we're looking for
so keep exploring
go far and wide
or go inside but go deep
        go deep
as if james cameron was filming a sequel to the abyss
and suddenly there was this location scout
trying to figure some way out
to get inside you
because you've been through hell and high water
and you went deep
keep exploring
because we are more
than a laundry list of things to do and places to see
     we are more than hills to ski
or countryside ponds to skate
we are the abandoned hesitation of all those who can't wait
we are first-rate greasy-spoon diners and healthy-living cafes
a country that is all the ways you choose to live
a land that can give you variety
because we are choices
we are millions upon millions of voices shouting
"keep exploring... we are more"
we are the surprise the world has in store for you
it's true
canada is the "what" in "what's new?"

so don't say "been there done that"
unless you've sat on the sidewalk
while chalk artists draw still lifes
on the concrete of a kid in the street
beatboxing to neil young for fun
don't say you've been there done that
unless you've been here doing it
let this country be your first-aid kit
for all the times you get sick of the same old same old
let us be the story told to your friends
and when that story ends
leave chapters for the next time you'll come back
               next time pack for all the things
you didn't pack for the first time
but don't let your luggage define your travels
each life unravels differently
and experiences are what make up
the colours of our tapestry
we are the true north
strong and free
and what's more
is that we didn't just say it
we made it be.

* Commissioned by the Canadian Tourism Commission

Help Wanted

Every day grandma would come into my room
and I'd hear her say
"rise and shine
the world has a window that holds a sign
there's help wanted out there somewhere
young man"
so I rose and I shone
I put on my shoes and I was gone

see grandma bought me my first phone
she said
"don't bother calling the people who care
call the people who don't
don't bother calling the people
who've taken up a fight
call the people who won't"

I learned at a very young age
where my grandma's rage came from
the entire congregation would nod
never ask grandma about god

I'd argue with her every day
all she'd say is
"go down to the store
buy some light bulbs
and when you run out
buy some more
because the light at the end of your tunnel
needs to be maintained

"you can't let it be stained
by 'their beliefs are better than your beliefs'
and you can't agree to disagree
because they're fucking wrong

"it's not the strong who've gotten lazy
but your vision is a little hazy
you're not sure what it is you want
when what you got is all you need
it falls to greed
for every hypocritical church-goer
who won't walk past the beggars
because they can't spare a dime"
grandma said "fuck them
I don't talk to god
because I ain't got the time"

and yeah
it struck me as strange
every time I walked past someone
who stopped me to ask
"can you spare some change?"
because yes I can
but I don't carry change
around in my back pocket
I don't wear it around my neck
on a chain in some locket
I keep change on the tip of my tongue
so I can climb the rung
of a ladder to a better place
I forgot about saving face
grandma told me "save your grace"

I keep change in the tip of my pen
and it seeps out every now and then
in spurts of angry ink
that make me think
maybe the writing on the wall
could use a little revision
grandma told me
"stop trying to calculate the difference
between people
people don't need division
gotta stick together
gotta love each other
father brother sister mother
uncles cousins aunts
forget about the chants and cheers
the jokes the jeers
after two thousand years
you'd think we'd know by now"
grandma said
"we will only find equality
in our number of tears"
and she was right
I don't know what injustices you've suffered
based on size sex race religion
or the political pigeon
shitting on the shoulders of us versus them
like in bethlehem
when a man said hey
I could be wrong
but can't we all just get along
no
so we nailed him to a tree

see justice isn't justice
it just is
and I can't change it
and you can't change it
so we gotta try to rearrange it
and I could offer you this miracle
a chance to see
a chance to see what I see
to see the way people see me
because if seeing is believing
and you see what I see
you wouldn't want to see anymore
but I've got a little surprise in store
for every man who looks upon me
with judgment in his eyes
there's a woman who looks upon me
with wetness in her thighs

I'm the world's greatest overweight lover
and you might just laugh
and you might just scoff
but my bones are made from sticks and stones
and names just piss me off

grandma told me
"young man you can't be concerned
with whatever it is they've got
the only reason they think they're beautiful
is the same reason
they think you're not
and young man
you have beauty beyond measure

you are a treasure entrenched in this earth
you can't let strangers determine your worth
rise and shine"

so I rose and I shone
I put on my shoes and I was gone
see grandma bought me my first phone
she said "young man
from time to time
I too need to smile
would you do me a favour and keep me
on speed dial?"

yes grandma
I will
and still to this day
I can call her up and hear her say
"it's a game
'you play you win
you play you lose
you play'
rise and shine
the world has a window that holds a sign
there's help wanted out there somewhere
but young man
if you are playing to win
the first thing you have to do
is apply within."

Skin 2

I don't imagine you
saran-wrapped in black latex
or seeping out the edges
of something tight and red

I don't close my eyes
to dream of your back
arched at the impossible angle
of a bow pulled tight
encouraging your shoulder blades
to drip the blood
of stockpiled broken hearts
but I hope the sound
of you not shielding your eyes
from my blinding humility
will one day top the charts

it's the most beautiful thing I've ever heard
and you're the charlie chaplin of your beautifuls
because you make me believe it
when you say it all without saying a word

looking at you it occurred to me
I could sit around all day
wearing nothing but your kiss

you make mirrors
want to grind themselves
back down into sand
because they can't do your reflection justice

and this just in
I am done with those
who in life would have made me fight
an army of imperfections
a battalion of flaws
tonight we're going to keep this city up
when they hear our bodies
slap together like applause.

Fallout Man

Fallout man sits stranded in a hotel room
like the last remaining survivor
of a nuclear war

all of a sudden
the hotel staff
becomes a band of mutants
pounding on his door and yelling
"would you like us to make your bed?"

he replies
"no thanks"
because he has seen the episodes
of bad science fiction sitcoms
where the triple-headed multi-armed monsters
try trickery to gain access
to a man's fallout shelter

he looks outside the window
and sees a man lugging his luggage
towards the hotel lobby
and finally realizes

"I am not the last man on earth"

stepping out of his fallout shelter
fallout man laughs a good morning
towards the young boy
who is shooting him
with a dollar-store potato gun

because the woman
who is far away
   the woman whose lips
will taste like home
after far too long on the road
   the woman with a butterfly net for hair
who has caught all of the falling stars
that he has spent his life wishing on

she has kissed him

he is not the last man on earth

and still she has kissed him.

These Hands

These hands were taught by a priest
taught that the least offensive thing they could do
would be to glue themselves together in prayer
but since I was only a child
I could never afford the postage fare
to get my words from here
to heaven

so by the age of eleven
these hands were beaten
beaten until my knuckles became indents
beaten until the smell of frankincense
made me sick
because these hands were beaten
with a metre stick
that they called their board of education
told me it was cut from the tree of knowledge
didn't have to go to college
to find out
that shit wasn't right
a church is no place
for a boy to have to learn how to fight
so I built my temple of worship
inside my mind
because all I could find
were these hatchets to bury
that blossomed into axes to grind
in my garden of even
leaving these hands
to find faith in someone like you

and it's true
I've never been one to keep myself rooted to the ground
but with you I've found
I'm like a flower
you're like a sun
you're the only one
who's worth straightening myself up for
I find myself shopping for advice
at an inconvenience store
where the more you buy
the more you need
and I'm seldom a man to fall victim to greed
but when it comes to you
I'm jealous of the whole world

jealous of the way the wind knocks at your window
asking if your hair can come out to play
jealous of the way the trees sway towards you
using their branches to knock away the birds
willing to sacrifice their beaks
to carve words into the wood
that could be interpreted
as recommendations
on how to turn these hands into foundations
strong enough to come together
and beg please
to all those trees
who held out their stories
about one-night loves and long-lasting stands
I've learned a hundred new tricks trying to please them
because somehow I thought
it was love they kept concealed in their hands

but these hands

if these fingertips had lips
they could kiss you with a touch
make love to you inside of a handshake
then take your hands
and read your palms like psalms
that would melt into scriptures
paint pictures
of octopi coming out of their caves
using their ink to tattoo the waves
with love poems
that would wash up on the shores
and stain the sands
while these hands took those sands
and sculpted sand castles
                    sand mansions
           and sand little-white-picket-fence homes
with those poems all decorating the walls
so every time you walked down the halls
you could read about how these hands
dream of becoming elastic bands
so they can stretch out towards you
and slingshot you back to me
we can sit and see
the dawn stretching into the dusk
and like ganesh
I could break off a tusk
write down my devotion to you
like a bible
with ten million different commandments
on how to make you happy

just so god would hold me liable
for every temple these hands built
for every bell tower these hands rung
for every song that was sung
by people who thought they could forget about me
and fight to see who could love you more
never realizing I could start my own private holy war
between these hands

my left is jealous of my right
when it becomes a prisoner trapped inside your hair
and my right is jealous of my left
when it finds that secret spot on your body
that prompts you to moan
which translates into "right there"
and these hands melt down like candles
as they slide down into your love I-can't-handles
they congeal into one solid mass
so that I can pray
that our relationship
becomes like those hurdles in grade-eight track class
we'll have to climb under each other
because god knows we could never get over each other
we'll sit across from one another
pondering each other's stories
and like children with abusive parents
we'll learn a hundred different ways to say I'm sorry
because we can't tell
who's holding whose hand a little too tight
and it might just be
that we will never grace the covers
of vogue or gq

but you make me feel beautiful
under a sun that shines only for supermodels
together we're two bottles
of really good booze
in a land where people choose not to drink
we're two bright ideas
in a world that doesn't want to think

so when my life flashes before my eyes
I don't want to see blue skies or shooting stars
I want to see pictures of all the nights
your lips became whips
and left me with scars
I want to see these hands
doing the least offensive thing they can do
I want to feel these hands
holding you.

Sketch

If I knew what I know now then
way back when we first met
I'd point to the sunset and say

I drew that for you

see

it's wrinkling in the rain.

No Need

I never truly
considered myself a man
until a woman called me
baby
and maybe
that's why we agreed to say
fare thee well love
with just a kiss

so you opened my mouth like an envelope
unfolded my tongue like a letter
studied my mind like it was the mail
as I played the blind man
with my fingers
feeling your goosebumps
fly south for the winter
I read your thoughts like braille

no need to search for answers
hidden somewhere
behind our eyes
because your thighs parted like the red sea
as your hand took my hand
became our hand
and I walked through
to find the promised land
collapsed on your body
like it was the desert
with my face in your sand
searching your curves for every secret oasis

places where our sweat collected
stealing sips of water till I was resurrected
your fingernails found bone beneath my skin
crucified me to your bed
and five times in one night
I rose from the dead

each time you turned to me and said
"if you need some love
I think I've got some you can borrow
and there's no need to pay it back
just be my friend tomorrow"

and suddenly our bodies remembered
how to move
like a favourite record
you listen to
over and over again
the needle found the groove
and the music we made
played upon our bones
like those fisher price xylophones
taking us back to our childhood
when we would smile at each other
and not care why

there was no need to find reasons
as we watched winter spring into summer
then fall
back into an endless cycle of seasons
we wondered when the weather would worsen
watching the wind work the water into waves

white squalls and whirlpools that would wage war
against all those relationships
trying to find a way through the storm
all those boys who promised reform
as they unzipped a young girl's dress
and that young girl stood there like equality
suffering through zero progress

but we secured ourselves in each other's stare
like my hair found anchors in your hair
the only storm we saw was
when god laid lightning down
between our lips
as if to say
"don't make me come down there"

I could write
ten more poems
just about the lightning
a million more about your lips
I felt my fingertips
grow into your hips
like I was taking root in your soil
like you became my earth
giving birth to my body
my bones breaking off into branches
building birdhouses for blue jays
becoming base camps for bees
my arms became trees
blossoming back into your hair
trying to tame
the dandelions blooming there

no need for you to say
I love you
because the way you were looking at me
I could already hear it
making my eyes roll back
inside of my head
looking within myself
I found my own spirit
you made me feel
like I could heal my own heart
and start to believe for the first time
without a clever rhythm or rhyme
that

I am beautiful

and because of that
you deserve a better fare thee well love than just a kiss
because of that
you deserve a better poem than this

but
we said fare thee well love
until our lips were numb
you lying on top of me
whispering I'm going now
but don't feel pressured to come

I shook my head
in that "no" sort of way

stay

there are flowers
that would volunteer themselves to die of thirst
just so they could offer you buckets of water
on hot summer days
and what are the chances we found each other
we're just two mice trapped with millions
in a really big maze

stay

until our yesterday becomes our today
and we can sculpt our tomorrow
out of the clay of everything
we never had a chance to say
but you shook your head
in that "no" sort of way
there was no need
to bend the silence into sound
no other way to say fare thee well love

because a kiss
was just more profound.

The Words You Have Written

You are holding this book
envisioning park benches
with reading lamps attached to them
so that people
can read your book at night
without fear of being mugged
all of the muggers
have stopped mugging
because people only carry your poems
in their purses and wallets
and use them to trade for food and shelter
                                    and love

you imagine school buses and hallways
falling silent
except for the sound of pages
being turned at the same time
and you smile
while thinking
about the white student
holding hands
with the black student
both offering their snack packs
to the yellow student
who is collecting food
for the red student
who is loved
by the yellow black and white students
who have all based their kindness
on the words you have written

and you want to believe
              believe that this book
should be taught in schools
              believe that this book
and its pages are made from the paper
of a tree that grew legs and walked away
from a mob of men in pointy white masks
then used its branches like arms
to hold another man
who was scared
              believe that this book
and its pages
are made of mirrors
              believe that this book
is holding you
and is flipping through your pages
reflecting your truths
reflecting you

you are holding this book
reading
the words you have written.

Move Pen Move

"Stay"
that's what mothers say
when their sons and daughters
go away
they say "stay"

my mother said "go"
so I wasn't there
the night she fell out of her wheelchair
so frustrated that she amputated
her own legs
or rather tried to
with a steak knife
her life leaking out
onto the white floor
blossoming like roses in the snow

our relationship was an anthem
composed of words like
"gotta go"

so we went
and sent our regards
on postcards
from all the places we'd been
with stories
about all the things we'd seen
that's how it was with you and I
why say goodbye
when we could still write

but then it took your hands
we should have practiced our goodbyes
because then it took your eyes

I was somewhere in the middle of nowhere
watching the sun rise over a stop sign
placed down the centre line of a highway
filled with sudden turns for the worse
running back home
because I gotta play nurse
        gotta figure out
which pill alleviates which pain
which part of your brain
was being used for a boxing bag
as your body
became a never-ending game
of freeze tag
taking place in an empty playground
I was left looking for your limbs
in a lost-and-found
and I couldn't set you free

so we just sat there
our heads bent towards each other like flowers
in the small hours of the morning
while light wandered in like a warning
that time is passing
and you right along with it
bit by bit every day
and all I could say was
"I would write you some way out of this
but my gift is useless"

and you said
"no
write me a poem to make me happy"

so I wrote
move pen move
write me a bedroom where cures
make love to our cancers

but my mother just motions to a bottle full of answers
and says
"help me go"
and now I know something of how a piano must feel
when it looks at the fireplace
to see sheet music
being used for kindling
smoke signalling the end of some song
that I thought it would take too long to learn
I just sit here watching you burn away
all those notes I never had a chance to play
to hear the music of what you had to say
but I count out the pills
only to see if I can do it
I can't even get halfway through it
before I turn back into your son and say
"stay"

I could hook up my heart to your ears
let my tears be your morphine drip
because maybe it's easier to let you slip away
than it is to say goodbye

so I hold my breath
because in the countdown to death
the question of why melts into when
how much time do we have left

because if I knew what I know now then
move pen move
write me a mountain

headstones are not big enough

my mother says
"stop it
write me a poem to make me happy"
so I write this

stay

she smiles and says
"gotta go"

I know

goodbye.

A Note from Shane

this note is a thank-you... to be honest, i don't say it enough.
my life has changed in so many beautiful and unexpected
ways this year. i've said farewell to so many extraordinary
people and it is the lessons of mortality that have disciplined
and tempered me beyond the narrow scope through which i
used to view this life. thank you to those who saw me through
it... thank you to those who tried. even now i am forced to
question my inability to make those around me feel beautiful,
loved, and appreciated. i have never excelled in the skill of gratitude,
the craft of gratefulness. but i need a mountaintop to
yell thank you from... for those who allowed their heart to be
the handle when i needed to get a grip, i shout "thank you"... to
the doctors and teachers... to the old and new lovers... to Sandy,
whose generosity staggers me beyond words... you are the
framework for the restoration of my faith... to the woman who
gave me this astonishing life... even as strangers we were never
on a first-name basis... i cherish you to the point of breaking
open and love you past what it takes to keep myself together...
to my grandmother... language simply fails. to the guiding
mother, the resting mother, and the mother who makes me
shine... may the volume of my gratitude echo until the birds
scatter and the world trembles before its humility.

The author would like to credit the following influences to his work. In **Restaurant**, the line "what you risk reveals what you value" is credited to Jeanette Winterson (The Passion). In **Help Wanted**, the line "you play you win/you play you lose/you play" is credited to Jeanette Winterson (The Passion) and Grandma. The poem **No Need** was strongly influenced by the work of Ani DiFranco. In **Move Pen Move,** the line "write me a mountain/ because headstones are not big enough" is credited to a similar line by Leonard Cohen.

Download mp3s of some of these poems at:
http://www.houseofparlance.com/VisitingHours/